# How to Survive
# A
# Home Purchase

## By

## Annie Acorn

## With

## Patrick Lee

Disclaimer and Terms of Use: No information contained in this book should be considered as physical, health related, financial, tax, or legal advice. Your reliance upon information and content obtained by you at or through this publication is solely at your own risk. The author assumes no liability or responsibly for damage or injury to you, other persons, or property arising from any use of any product, information, idea, or instruction contained in the content provided to you through this book.

# INTRODUCTION

Let us start right off the bat by admitting that this book has NOT been written by a realtor, a mortgage broker, a lawyer, a home inspector, an appraiser, or a contractor.

Patrick has successfully followed a career in business with a sideline in training for a number of years. Annie has owned several successful businesses and is a successful author, editor, and publisher. Together they once successfully flipped a retail company that included two owned stores and three franchised stores.

Between them they have purchased several homes through conventional mortgages, but recently, Patrick decided to live a bit on the wild side.

Recognizing that there were some real bargains available in the currently down real estate market and wishing to cash in on this, Patrick located a house that needed MAJOR improvements. His plan all along was to "flip" the house, so that he could live in it comfortably himself.

Early on in the process, he searched the web for information that would provide guidance, but what he found instead was horror story after horror story.

Undaunted, he moved ahead with his plans, bringing his overall business knowledge and past experience along with him.

Amazingly, for him the experience was trouble free.

One by one, the professionals he encountered mentioned that his purchase was going smoothly, while others before him had floundered. When asked by Patrick for a possible explanation for his success in the face of other's failures, several of the professionals offered valuable insights as to why.

To both Patrick and Annie, it appeared that another collaboration was in order. After all, no home is perfect. Many of them require updates or changes to accommodate the needs of new occupants. At the very least, most of them need "freshening up," usually well beyond just a few coats of paint. The result is this book, *How To Survive Your New Home Purchase.*

Read carefully, take notes, don't be afraid to ask questions, and you, too, will look back at a successful home purchase.

# SELECTING A PROPERTY

After living in his first house for many years, Patrick recognized that the market was hot and his neighborhood was changing. To him this seemed like a no brainer, and he put his house on the market, sold it, moved in with a friend, and began looking around for a new house to purchase.

Two months later, the market began to nosedive. Not wishing to overspend, Patrick continued to save towards his down payment, while keeping tabs on the ever changing market around him.

During the next year, he systematically viewed over one hundred houses – some historic, some new construction, and some foreclosures. None of them felt quite like home – that is until he viewed one two doors down from the friend's house, where he was currently living.

Patrick would have been hard pressed to explain exactly why this house appealed to him, but it did.

True, it sat on a lovely lot overlooking a lake in a nice neighborhood with which he was already familiar. The school district was excellent, which was good for eventual resale. The house had hardwood floors, a new roof, and new thermal pane windows, but that is where the good news ended.

The previous owners had inherited a house from a relative two years before and immediately moved, abandoning the property in which Patrick was now interested.

In the intervening two years, vandals had taken the outside heat pump unit, all the copper pipes that connected the water heater (located in the crawl space as is common in the South) to the house, and pulled loose the electrical box from the outside wall. In addition, the house had been built in the '70s, and the wiring was no longer up to code.

These things alone would have caused most people to run, but Patrick hung on, recognizing that the house had good bones.

The floors were solid, and the home's overall layout flowed nicely. Someone had erected a bank of unneeded cabinets between the living room and the kitchen, but these could be easily removed – a step that would result in a more open concept. The kitchen was dirty, but cleaned up it would be functional. The bathrooms needed some upgrading, but again, once cleaned, would be functional. New living room carpet and kitchen flooring were givens, and every wall and door in the house needed painting.

There were two large storage buildings in the backyard that needed to be removed from the property. Someone had also added an unnecessary deck onto the back, but this could be easily removed and lumber from it used to repair the bigger deck that added to the house's value.

Over the years, Patrick and some of his buddies (a few of whom actually worked in the construction business) often got together on Saturdays and helped one another with DIY projects around their respective houses. Now it would be his turn, and he felt that a few weeks of hard work would return the house to its original beauty.

So…

Patrick contacted a realtor and put in an offer, based on all the work that needed to be done to make the house livable.

A day passed, then a week, then a month…

Two months later, he finally received a response. The owners had come down on their price, but not nearly enough.

It was clear that the two parties were too far apart to come to terms with each other. Disappointed, Patrick resumed his search, continuing to keep his finger on the pulse of the overall market.

Overpriced, the house continued its lonely vigil as it looked over the lake, a "Price Reduced" sign was added to its front yard, and its shrubbery grew.

Four months later, Patrick rechecked the home's listing, as he had done every week since he had taken back his offer, and noted that a second price reduction had been made. The house was now listed for the amount of his first offer.

He reached out his hand and dialed his realtor's phone number.

## SELECTING A REALTOR

Over the years, Patrick had worked with a number of realtors, some of them better than others.

Some were too pushy.  Others didn't know their own market.

As a single male, he occasionally found realtors, who didn't seem to understand that his wants were different from the needs of a family.

One realtor had listed the first home he had sold with no intention of ever showing it, only needing an additional listing to satisfy his own broker's monthly requirement.  After two months of no activity, Patrick had severed the relationship with no problem.

Working with a realtor that was representing both parties had also resulted in a bad experience.

Hoping that things would go smoothly, he created a list of qualities that he felt were essential to a good working relationship with a realtor.

1). The realtor must have a certain level of experience, preferably more than two years.

2). The realtor must belong to a well established firm of some size.

3). The realtor must have extensive knowledge of homes listed in the area of interest to the purchaser.

4). The realtor must be able to recommend a certified home inspector.

5). The realtor must be an able negotiator, not too wary of taking a chance, and willing to walk away from a deal if the sellers refuse to meet the purchaser's target figures.

6). The realtor must be able to recommend qualified, licensed contractors in all areas of home repair.

7). The realtor must be conversant with a broad range of mortgage brokers.

8). The realtor must be knowledgeable about all types of financing opportunities that are available to the real estate purchaser in today's market.

**And last, but not least:**

**9). The realtor must answer all phone numbers given and respond to any and all emails received.**

List in hand, Patrick now went back through the names of those realtors, who had been helpful to him in the past.

Since he had viewed over one hundred properties, there were quite a few of them, some of which were easily removed from consideration.

Once his list of possibilities dropped into the single digits, any of them would have done nicely, so Patrick started phoning. The first one that he actually reached was deemed the winner. Her name, for purposes of this book, will be Sally.

Sally met all of the criteria. She was a pleasant woman in her forties, who had sold real estate for many years and was attached to a large, well-advertised firm. Her specialty was the area in which Patrick lived and his prospective home was listed, and she had shown him several properties previously that he had liked.

Her manner was cordial, but not overly friendly. She was not pushy. She obviously knew her stuff and had previously offered a number of helpful suggestions. As the old country song says, "She knew when to old 'em and when to fold 'em."

Patrick felt they were well suited. He made an appointment.

# MAKING AN OFFER

That evening Patrick met with his new real estate BFF, Sally, and they hit it off immediately. He liked her direct, no nonsense approach, and she respected him for garnering a better purchase price by having walked away from an unsatisfactory purchase negotiation earlier.

Patrick outlined his expectations:

**1). Offer amount – LESS THAN ASKING.**

**2). Seller to pay ALL closing costs.**

**3). Earnest money to be offered - MINIMUM.**

**4). Home inspection requirement – DO NOT PURCHASE A HOME, EVEN A NEW HOME, WITHOUT ONE!!!**

**5). Mortgage final approval clause – Patrick was already preapproved.**

**6). Reasonable date set for closing.**

**7). Septic tank inspection to be paid for by Seller.**

**8). Termite and other critter inspection to be paid for by Seller.**

Sally completed the necessary documents and provided them to Patrick for review.

Patrick **took the time to review the documents** and **then** signed.

Sally provided Patrick with copies of the signed documents and accepted his check for the earnest money.

Patrick went home, and Sally submitted the offer.

It was a Friday evening, and both of them prepared to wait. They didn't have to wait long.

The realtor, who had listed the house, made two half-hearted attempts to show it to other perspective buyers over the weekend, but with the power turned off and the odors from the house having been closed up for so long trailing along with them, neither party stayed inside for more than a few minutes.

How do we know this? Because Patrick and his friend had their eyes glued to a telescope strategically placed in front of the friend's dining room window – just kidding, but close.

Monday evening, Patrick had just finished dinner when Sally called to inform him of the other realtor's response. Both Patrick and Sally were surprised by its contents.

Perhaps Patrick's walking away from the deal four months before had made more of a difference than they had realized. Neither of them will ever know, and frankly, neither of them cares.

The Sellers had accepted Patrick's offer as presented – no ifs, ands, or buts about it.

Patrick was now well on the way to buying a home.

# A 203K MORTGAGE

Given the size of the basic repairs that were needed to make Patrick's proposed home livable, Sally agreed that a 203K Mortgage would be the financing vehicle that was needed, and so Patrick prepared to move forward in this direction.

He had already done some basic research on the subject, but he now proposed to do more.

The U. S. Department of Housing and Urban Development defines the 203K mortgage as "HUD's primary program for the rehabilitation and repair of single family properties." on its website. The website further states that, "As such, it is an important tool for community and neighborhood revitalization and for expanding homeownership opportunities."

Why is the FHA 203K mortgage program so necessary? Simply stated, it's because of all of the foreclosed properties that are glutting the market.

Owners of foreclosed properties are by definition frustrated, angry, and broke. Many of them strip the houses of everything from appliances to floor coverings to bathroom fixtures before the mortgage holder takes them over.

In the old days, back when real estate was booming, these houses would have been looked at primarily by "flippers." Such flippers can do a good job, but many of them are only in it for the money and seem to take little, if any, pride in their work. The resultant "repairs," therefore, are often substandard, done without permits and/or inspections, and occasionally are outright dangerous to the new homeowner.

In today's market, buyers like Patrick have become much more savvy, realizing that they may do a better job of "flipping" a home themselves, especially if they wish to live in it as opposed to turning a quick profit.

Basically, an FHA 203K mortgage provides the buyer with a single mortgage that encapsulates two parts:

**1). Part 1** – Covers the purchase price of the house, which must still be within the FHA approved mortgage limit for the area.

**2). Part 2 -** Covers necessary repairs that have been submitted to and approved by the mortgage holder during the approval process. The cost of these repairs must be at least $5,000.00 and less than $35,000.00.

The total dollar amount of both parts added together must remain within the FHA approved mortgage limit for the area, given the home's new upgraded value.

This means that the home must undergo two appraisals – one to determine that the home in its current, non-refurbished condition is worth at least as much as the dollars being lent to the purchaser under Part 1 and the second to determine that the value of the home after all repairs have been completed will be at least as much as the dollar amount being lent to the purchaser under both Part 1 and Part 2 added together.

The purpose of this book is to outline how you can negotiate your way through a home purchase and rehabilitation, utilizing a 203K mortgage. For more information about the FHA 203K mortgage itself, both Annie and Patrick recommend that you visit the U. S. Department of Housing and Urban Development website at:
http://portal.hud.gov/hudportal/HUD?src=/program_offices/housing/sfh/203k/203kmenu .

## SELECTING A BROKER

When selecting a broker, KNOWLEDGE ISN'T EVERYTHING.

No, we are not saying that it isn't necessary for the broker that you choose to be VERY knowledgeable about all types of mortgages.

We would recommend that you steer completely clear of any mortgage broker who isn't extremely knowledgeable about any mortgage program that you are considering.

Someone's uncle, cousin, or the guy along the street, who has been out of work for three years and is now trying something new, are not going to be your best bets here.

But still, there is another variable that plays into the smooth flow of your overall home purchase.

When you chose your real estate agent, you picked the first member of your home purchase team.  In

Patrick's case, he chose Sally, so let's think of her as his pitcher.

If your real estate agent is your pitcher, then your mortgage broker is your catcher. If the two of them don't communicate and work well together, you – the coach – will lose the game or, if you are extremely lucky, pull out a tie. You certainly will never look back on this home purchase and think of yourself as a winner. The road to completion will have been way too rocky.

Most experienced real estate agents have developed a nice list of mortgage brokers, who they have found to be professional, ethical, and calm in a storm.

Ask for this list, and discuss the pros and cons of each one mentioned on it with your realtor. Really listen. If you hear the slightest hesitation in your realtor's voice, then that one is no longer under consideration.

Buying a home is one of the most stressful things a person can do, having to deal with your real estate agent and your mortgage broker constantly being at each other's throats is not something that you want to add to the mix.

Once you have narrowed this list down, then meet with the mortgage brokers that remain on the list, because it is equally important that you can get along with them as they ask for one piece of financial documentation after another and you wait long hours for important decisions to be made.

As you may recall, Patrick had already been preapproved for a mortgage when his own home purchase process started. We would always recommend preapproval to any potential home buyer.

After all, why would you want to look at and get your hopes up about homes in the $2,000,000.00 price range, when your budget will only allow you to buy a home in the $200,000.00 price range?

As it turned out, Patrick's preapproval was through a mortgage broker with whom Sally already worked well, so there was no problem.

While it may slow down the initial stages of your buying process, it is generally best to line up your real estate agent and your mortgage broker prior to looking at properties. After all, you wouldn't start a game without a healthy pitcher and catcher in place.

# THE HOME INSPECTION

It's impossible for us to stress too much that you should NEVER, NEVER, NEVER EVER purchase a house without a home inspection.

It doesn't matter if the home you are purchasing is a historic Victorian, a mid-century modern, or a new construction – GET IT INSPECTED!  Even if it's the house right next door to your current home and you've been in it a million times, GET IT INSPECTED!  Even if it's the house you grew up in GET IT INSPECTED!

Are you getting our drift?

Think of this member of your team as your short stop.

If the house doesn't do well when inspected, you will want to stop play and reevaluate.  You may continue with the purchase, but your eyes will now be opened and your realtor may need to step in and negotiate new terms.

A good home inspector will look way beyond outward appearances. He/she will go up on the roof, into the attic, and through the crawl space. You know, the places were no sane man or woman has gone before.

Home inspectors also know and understand current building codes and construction material trends.

If you are purchasing an older house, codes have almost certainly changed since its construction. Wiring and plumbing, as well as heating and air, could easily need serious updating to meet your area's building code requirements, which is important. These codes are put into place for you and your family's protection. They keep you safe, while you sleep at night.

If you are purchasing a new construction home, a good home inspector will recognize shoddy workmanship that may be hidden under glossy cosmetic appearances.

House hunting is a long and arduous process, and buyers are often tantalized into seeing that which they wish to see. Those may be hardwood floors under your feet, but did you realize that the builder used the thinnest flooring available? This may not seem terribly important right now, but if you ever have a need to sand and refinish those floors, you will think otherwise.

Notice that we keep referring to a "good" home inspector. As with most other things, there are good and bad home inspectors.

An experienced real estate agent can usually supply you with a list of inspectors that they know are knowledgeable, experienced, and thorough. Don't be afraid to ask your realtor, "If this was your house, which one of these inspectors would you use?"

Notice the word thorough in the description above. A thorough home inspection can easily take several hours.

If at all possible be at the house, when the inspector is there. This may well be some of the best time you ever invest in a project.

A good inspector can show you item by item the home's pros and cons. He/she can give you probable costs and options for needed repairs, as well as likely remaining lifespans for such things as the roof.

You may not have noticed that the house's hot water heater is located directly over the bathtub in which your children will be bathing, but your inspector will.

Furthermore, he/she will realize that it isn't properly supported.

If you're on the spot at the time, you and your inspector can discuss various options, such as increasing the unit's support, moving it to another location, or changing over to a tankless system, and each option's probable costs. Such knowledge can be invaluable when you and your real estate agent discuss the situation and renegotiate terms with the seller later.

Once the inspection is completed, you are equipped to prioritize and justify the repairs that you want done prior to closing. Now it's time to talk money.

# PREPARING FOR THE PROCESS

You are now on the fifty yard line to mix our analogies.  You have selected your pitcher, your catcher, and your short stop.  You have located the house of your dreams, although right now it looks a little unloved.

STOP!  Take a deep breath, and PREPARE!

Most of us would be ashamed for anyone else to see the state of our financial papers, so don't be embarrassed.  Believe us, though, when we say that it is definitely the time for you to get your ducks in a row, and we're not talking about your credit score here.

We're assuming that you have already been preapproved for your mortgage.  Even so, having all of your financial papers dumped into the same box is not going to be sufficient.

A tax return that's completed from a shoe box full of yearly receipts and records probably isn't going to result in the largest return.  By the same token, a mortgage application process that is gone into with a hodge-podge of estimates and financial documents, probably isn't going to go smoothly.

Think in terms of two parts to this process – securing estimates for the repairs that are needed on the house and organizing your own personal financial records.  Either part, if not adequately prepared, can cause unnecessary delays and impact closing deadlines.

Let's start with the estimates.

In Patrick's case, the house he was purchasing needed serious electrical, plumbing, and HVAC work – well beyond anything that he and his DIY friends could do.  The kitchen cabinets and counters could be upgraded later, but the kitchen appliances were outdated, filthy, and quite possibly dangerous.  These four items, then, comprised his wish list for immediate repair after closing.

Patrick proceeded to secure estimates on the repairs, having first taken advice again from his realtor.  Any experienced real estate agent will know which area contractors can be counted on to show up and do quality work for a reasonable price.

In each case he:

1).  Made sure that the contractor to be used was currently licensed, bonded, and insured.

2).  Made sure that the contractor understood the work would be done immediately after Patrick's closing on the house.

3).  Made sure that the contractor understood that Patrick wanted the work completed within one week after closing.

4).  Made sure that the contractor understood that the estimate had to be complete and final, i.e. there could be no surprises as to cost after work began, because the amount borrowed to cover the repairs could not be revisited.

5).  Made sure that the contractor provided him with an itemized written estimate that outlined all work to be done and any guarantees offered by the contractor.

As for the appliances, Patrick's searched all types of options, including close-outs and sales.  Picking out the appliances ahead of time, enabled Patrick to shop more leisurely and take advantage of some real bargains.

This brings us to what, for some, is the harder part.

If you want your mortgage application experience to go smoothly, then you MUST have your bank statements, tax returns, credit card information, and secondary/investment income statements organized and be prepared to present them at a moment's notice.

Do we really need to stress here that keeping yourself in good graces with your mortgage broker is always a good idea?

In Patrick's case, whenever he was asked for a document, he provided his mortgage broker with two copies – a small thing, you might think, but a gesture that the broker appreciated.

Patrick also made it a point to provide the requested materials as quickly as possible. On occasion, this required him to spend most of a lunch hour in an automobile, but once again, his broker saw and appreciated the effort to comply with requests that Patrick was making.

From the broker's standpoint, in most instances, he was receiving the information that he needed, while Patrick's case file was still available and open on his desk.

From Patrick's standpoint, this allowed his request to proceed quickly and smoothly towards its ultimate conclusion without any question of there being a negative effect on the scheduled closing date.

Not meeting a closing date can, in some instances, cause a sale to go sour, and no buyer wants that to happen.

It is not uncommon for a broker's request to seem unnecessary or even unreasonable to the uninitiated. At some point, though, you have to trust your broker to know what he/she is doing, and we would recommend that you meekly provide him/her with whatever documentation he/she requires.

An experienced, ethical broker has absolutely no reason to want to tie up either your time and energy or his/her own. Give him or her what they ask for, as quickly and completely as possible, and move on.

# WHEN TO PRESS

Now that you have hurried up and provided your broker with the repair estimates, purchase invoices, and financial documents that he or she needs, you are entering the hard time.  Now you wait.

And you wait…

And you wait some more…

Sooner than later, the question will enter your mind, "When do I call him or her for an update?"

First of all, it is important to remember that your broker wants you to succeed.  Most of them have monthly completion goals to meet, and if you chose a broker that you felt was simpatico, then he likes you.

Second of all, it is important to remember that the squeaky wheel usually gets oiled first in our fast paced, high tech world.

The challenge is to find the middle ground in between.

When Patrick reached the point where he felt it was impossible for him to wait any longer for an update, he opted to email his broker.

He started with a brief sentence thanking his broker for guiding him through the process so far, and then he simply stated that he was checking in to see if there was anything else the broker needed from him at this time.

It is important to note that Patrick kept his email short, pleasant, and professional.

The response from his broker was received in less than an hour and was equally pleasant and professional. It was a simple assurance that the broker had everything he needed from Patrick and that things were progressing smoothly.

This wasn't much, but it was enough.

Patrick waited another week, but then, because he had set a fairly short contract to closing deadline, he felt it was necessary to check in again.

This time, he started by apologizing for bothering the broker again, but could he (the broker) please confirm that they final approval process for his mortgage approval was on target to meet the early closing date? Then he thanked the broker for his help and guidance through the process.

Again, Patrick's email was brief, pleasant, and professional, even though he was beginning to be a bit concerned about meeting the closing date.

Again, his brokers responded quickly with an assurance that everything was proceeding smoothly and meeting the closing would be no problem.

Patrick gritted his teeth and waited one more week. At this point, he was really concerned about meeting the rapidly approaching closing date. He picked up the phone.

Once the call was connected, he introduced himself and asked how his broker was doing. Upon receiving assurances that his broker was fine, Patrick pointed out that his closing date was rapidly approaching and that he was really concerned about their being able to make it.

Luckily, his broker was able to confirm that all was well.

The paperwork had been returned to the broker that day, and the required appraisal had come back well above the amount of Patrick's mortgage amount.

Patrick's mortgage was completely approved.

All that was left now was to actually close on the house, and the attorney, who had been recommended to handle the closing by both Patrick's realtor and his broker, had already been notified, and the date and time of the closing had already been set.

If you think of the appraiser and the attorney as Patrick's outfielders, his team had really come through for him. He could breathe again.

## GETTING YOUR CONTRACTORS INSPIRED

Once the closing was behind him, Patrick couldn't wait to get started.

As you will recall, he had been careful to select experienced, licensed contractors, who had been recommended by his realtor.

He had also taken time with each of them, explaining the time constraints imposed by his wanting to move into the house quickly and exactly when he expected the work to be done.

The week before, he had contacted each of his three contractors – think of them as his three basemen - and set appointments for their work to begin.

As soon as the keys were in his hands, he contacted each of the contractors again and arranged to take each of them keys to the house for ready access at their convenience.

He further made sure they each knew the names of the other contractors and the dates when each had agreed to perform work, so that they were all aware of the importance of their coordinating their efforts. As often happens with experience professionals, they all knew and had worked well with each other in the past, and Patrick felt that this also helped to keep things moving forward smoothly.

Within four days, all the work was completed, and the contractor's final checks were handed over.

Things couldn't have gone better. Why? Because Patrick:

**1). Had taken care when selecting his contractors in the first place.**

**2). Had been clear and up front about when the work was to be done.**

**3). Had touched based with his contractors prior to closing and set appointments for their work to be completed.**

**4). Oversaw much of the work personally and kept each contractor apprised of the progress being made by the others.**

**5). Made sure the contractors knew the date and the reason for the deadline and were inspired to meet it for one simple reason – their final payment.**

Once the contracted work was completed and the contractors had been paid, Patrick arranged for delivery and installation of his new appliances.

The electrical now met code and the water heater and HVAC system were properly connected and working. The extra bank of kitchen cabinets had been removed by Patrick and his friends, and the house had been thoroughly cleaned. The two large sheds had been sold and hauled off by a gentleman that Patrick had located on Craig's List, who had paid $2,000.00 for the privilege of owning what Patrick considered to be junk. The main two rooms had been painted, and the rest of the house had been primed. The living room carpet and kitchen flooring had both been replaced.

A huge difference had been made in a couple of weeks.

Since Patrick had opted to use an FHA 203K mortgage, his home now received a final FHA inspection. The inspector/appraiser now felt that the house would easily appraise for 25% more than Patrick had paid for it, including the upgrades and repairs.

Patrick couldn't have done better, and we both wish you the same success if you choose to purchase a new home for yourself and your family in this ever changing real estate environment.

# OTHER TITLES AVAILABLE FROM ANNIE ACORN PUBLISHING LLC

## By Annie Acorn

### *Chocolate Can Kill*

### *Murder With My Darling*

### *A Stranger Comes to Town*

### *When to Remain Silent*

### *On the Road*

### *The Magic Sand Dollar*

### *One More Christmas Past*

### *One Last Gift To Go*

### *A Tired Older Woman: Loses Weight and Keeps It Off!*

### *How to Survive A Home Purchase*

### *How to Survive Your 203K Mortgage*

## By Beverly J. Crawford

*My Mom Is Ruining My Life*

*A B-17 Christmas*

*The Christmas Child*

*Towards the Sun*

By denise hays

*Niki Knows the Dirt – A Niki Edgar Mystery*

*Walking for Weight Loss*

By Peggy Teel

*God and Grandma*

By Juliette Hill

*Pink Lemonade Diary*

All titles also available for NOOK!

## ABOUT ANNIE

Annie Acorn is the pseudonym of a prolific, internationally recognized author, whose readership recognizes her mainly for her cozy mysteries and richly woven stories with a warm southern flair. She is a founding member of From Women's Pens – A Cooperative of Women Writers.

Annie is the mother of two sons, one of whom ismarried to the best daughter-in-law in the world. She lives in the Washington, D.C. area, where she has done technical writing for AHRQ, NIH, HHS and SAMHSA.

She owned a tri-state medical outsourcing business for a number of years and was the Director of a behavioral healthcare firm. She once flipped a comic book and collectible retail company comprised of five stores, and she has managed cemeteries and funeral homes.

Ms. Acorn has published in The Inspirational Writer, and she edited an in-house publication for the State of Mississippi. She is a founding member of From Women's Pens – A Cooperative of Women Writers.

In her spare time, Ms. Acorn enjoys reading, writing mysteries, listening to classical music, playing cards, and spending time with her friends – usually at a restaurant serving delicious food.

www.ingramcontent.com/pod-product-compliance
Lightning Source LLC
Chambersburg PA
CBHW071545170526
45166CB00004B/1557